Crossing Paths

A Poetic Journey in 45 Days

Rick Van de Poll, Ph.D.

Illustrated by Tamara Viskovic

September, 2017

Copyright © Owl Feather Press, LLC

Rick Van de Poll, Ph.D. 2017

All rights reserved. No part of this publication may be reproduced, distributed, or transmitted in any form or by any means, including photocopying, recording, or other electronic or mechanical methods, without prior written permission of the publisher, except in the case of brief quotations embodied in reviews and certain other non-commercial uses permitted by copyright law.

Although the author and publisher have made every effort to ensure that the information in this book was correct at the time of publishing, the author and the publisher do not assume and hereby disclaim any liability to any party for any loss, damage, or disruption caused by errors or omissions, whether such errors or omissions result from negligence, accident, or any other cause.

ISBN No.: 978-0-9994808-1-6

This Book is dedicated to all of those people who encouraged me to go out into the woods and get lost from time to time, and to my wife who insisted that I come back in and write about it.

Table of Contents

Introduction 7

An Owl Came Calling Today 10

On The Improbability of Being (SO LOUD!!! Shhh…) 12

That Look In Your Eyes 14

'Conglomer-rock' 16

Emergence 18

Earth Day 20

The Vernal Pool 24

Fairy Shrimp 26

Ancient Paths 28

A Sad Rain 30

Wood Pile Serenade 32

Climate Change 34

A Cedar's Tale 36

A Great Weight 38

Lichen it or Not 40

The Last Mastodon 42

Spring Color 46

Tree Ring Story 48

Wilderness Lost 52

Black-throated Green Warbler 54

A Winter Wind 56

The Great Unfurling 58

Two Bears Came Running By 60

The Mystique of Morels.. 64

Greening of the Earth 66

Following the Path 68

Sitting on a Rock.. 70

A Warm Breeze.. 74

The First Baptism... 76

Incoming Storm 78

La Chanson du Pissenlit... 80

The Veery and the Thrush 82

Tree Story 84

Discrimination 86

Copperhead Creed... 90

Achieving Yellow 92

Coast Coming In 94

The Mystique of Morels II... 96

Fluttering Mud... 98

Just When You Thought... 100

Peek-a-boo Porky.. 104

Bluebird Wake-up Call... 108

The Four Kings.. 110

Tracking Sense.. 114

Journeying On... 118

Conclusion 123

Acknowledgments.. 125

About the Author.. 127

Introduction

This book of poetry is an expression of nature as seen from the eyes of someone who has devoted his entire life to the service of the natural world. Graced at an early age with an opportunity to be in nature every summer, "Dr. V," as his middle school students called him, has been fortunate enough to witness the miracle of natural life during all seasons of the year, both as a professional and as an advocate for the environment. He has studied the intricacies of all forms of life, from the microscopic to the global. With degrees in Outdoor Education, Environmental Communication, Mycology & Lichenology, and Natural Resource Management, the author has learned from some of the best field naturalists in the country, and studied with some of the most pre-eminent scientists of the 20th century.

Admittedly, most of the author's 'ah-ha' moments in nature has come while studying on his own. In fact, the author was already an accomplished botanist and birder before he entered college. While many of his high school friends were listening to music, going to the city, or partying with friends, Rick was off in some of the wildest spots he could find to walk, observe, and take note of the natural world around him.

The author brings a unique perspective to nature poetry. Born of a mission to both educate and inform, these poems have arisen from daily encounters with wild things. Each poem carries with it a back-story that sheds light on the context of the event, and allows the reader to understand how a particular observation triggered a flow of thought. The poem itself provides a counterpoint to the message by accentuating certain words and phrases. The cadence of the dialogue underscores the ecological value of selected aspects of each scene.

Tamara Viskovic beautifully illustrates these scenes with her own interpretation of the poem. With limited guidance from the author, she has created a collage of impressions, each pertinent to the poem and each poignantly depicting the essence of the observation. The sketches are both moving and concise, as if they arose from the words on the page themselves. Most importantly, they provide a window frame for the imagery of each poem, through which the reader can imagine even greater detail, color, and movement.

The end result is a daily journal of poems that at once provides insight into a fascinating realm of ecology, and offers a unique perspective on some of the most pressing threats to our natural world in this age. From shifting weather patterns to the loss of iconic wildlife species, to the general warming of our climate, this poetry collection underscores the need for all of us to pay more attention to that which has sustained through countless generations of life—the natural ecosystems of the Earth. It is the hope of the author that this small contribution to nature writing will act as a reminder that we shouldn't ever forget our responsibility as a species to act as conscientious stewards in caring for the planet.

Rick Van de Poll, Ph.D.

September 2017

An Owl Came Calling Today

An owl came calling today
Not any kind of owl
But one that stopped me dead in my tracks.
You see a headless, dead owl in the middle of the woods is
    not something I have ever seen before –
In my sixty years of wandering.
I recall a time, though, just yesterday perhaps,
I watched the light of an owl's eyes fade in my lap –
"I tried to miss him," my friend said, "Honest!" no doubt
    while taking a nap
Behind a two-ton cold steel killer of all in its path.
But this one was different, this bundle of down,
This pile of feather and fly,
This one was already gone, no head to be found, no glow in
    its eyes,
Still warm as I nestled it in my arms, just like this,
Warm, still warm as a summer's kiss.
If it weren't for that particular turn in my path,
And that sharp-bladed stone I had picked up minutes before
    – Why? just because, for without
I would not be walking home with a gift of wing,
A gift of impossibly light bone, sinew, and string,
An answer to a prayer not two weeks ago, when,
Stopped dead in my tracks, I came upon this headless
    thought,
"I need an owl wing today to tell my story,
To honor my ancestors,

To listen to the silence,
To hear them say, and say, and say,"
I heard an owl came calling today.

This poem was inspired by an encounter with a dead, headless owl in the woods. It lay there, still warm to the touch, right in the middle of the path. It was hard to tell what had caused its demise, although other than having no head, there was no obvious injury. No feathered or furry predator had plucked its feathers or disgorged it for eating. It laid perfectly calm and still, as if waiting for me to approach, pick it up, and ask for feather and wing. I laid down tobacco as was taught to me by my forefathers, and took the sharp stone that I had found a few minutes earlier, and worked away at removing its wing. It came cleanly, although with some effort at cutting sinew and tendon. The weight was extremely light, the wind it made was silent as the dead of night. I have used that wing ever since in ceremony and have always honored my owl brother for such a remarkable gift.

On The Improbability of Being
(SO LOUD!!! Shhh...)

Away in the night
Somewhere without light,
A peeper hazards a chirp – more like a burp,
An afterthought, after much mealing.
Then comes the moment,
That silence will foment,
A gathering refrain,
A reptilian insane,
Ten thousand peeps a-pealing.
My mind split asunder,
Noise way worse than thunder,
No thought, voice, or hush,
Can keep from the rush,
A wretched raucous recalcitrant reeling.
How can this be?
Issued from that I can't see,
So tiny, so small as I'm kneeling,
Down in the muck,
From whence I get stuck,
In search of this giant who's dealing,
A blow to my brain,
Now *I* am insane,
To stay here so long without stealing
Even the slightest of glances
At this giant of trances
In which I have lost total feeling!

This poem was the direct result of one of the countless times I have stood next to a vernal pond in spring and listened to chorusing peepers. For those readers who have done this, I need not explain. For those who haven't, I can only encourage you to put this on your "bucket list." The sound can be utterly deafening yet primally satisfying. From an impossibly small organism issues one of the loudest noises of the woods, an ear-splitting, mind-numbing cacophony that makes a single frog sound like dozens upon dozens. The ventriloqual effect of these tiny creatures is quite effective, especially if you're advertising for mates and want to show off your vocal prowess. A quick step or splash and all frogs hush quiet again, waiting, just waiting for the first brave soul to chirp, squeak, then peep. The sound begets more to join in and before long, without a thought to the danger that is present, the entire chorus arises again to a deafening crescendo. It's always amazing how *long* they can keep it up, all night as far as I can tell. Hard to imagine screaming at the top of your lungs for two or three weeks, let alone a single day!

That Look In Your Eyes

Wild
Knowing
Wondering
Gaze.
That look in your eyes,
A storied play.
For my part I was just standing there, waiting, watching
You're the one who led your family into danger
You're the one who took the leap
You're the one who didn't see me standing there,
All ablaze in orange, mouth agape
I could have kissed you, you were so close,
There was no escape.
But this watcher was not your usual fare,
No gun in hand, no pompous air.
I was but a mere onlooker, like you
Feeling the spring woods beneath my feet, finally snow-free
From winter's heartbeat.
I, like you, stood there in wonder, how did we meet?
Once upon a path, mine stationery, yours fleet,
At issue here is the taking of meat.
No, no predator am I today
So no need to run away from your biology, your progeny,
      your evolutionary seat.
No, today you foiled the follower, four-legged and neat
Today you lived another day, so be calm, rest easy say I,
All will be told in the blink of an eye.

This poem was inspired by a close encounter with a small family group of deer, who, by some small miracle, had little idea of who they would run into as they bounded away from some unseen predator. It was clear, after looking into the matriarch's eyes, that she had little intention of bringing her kin into more danger. Yet there she stood, just feet away, with that wild, wondering look. The two smaller deer stood staring at me as well, waiting, and watching the old one for cues. After what seemed an improbable amount of time the oldest gave a quick flick of the tail and moved off, slowly, cautiously, but having decided that it was safer to walk rather than flee. Whoever the other predator was also decided that a chase was not worth pursuing. We all left quietly on our way through the woods once again.

'Conglomer-rock'

Head cheese,
That marvelous invention of the Sixties,
In the era of Beach Boys, Beatles and Twinkies,
That 'Let's-get-rich-quick-on-the junk-we-can't-sell' if you
    please,
Largely unidentifiable brainy bits, sliced into a mashed up
    matrix of miscellaneous meats.
There it was before me, on the ground, everywhere. Or so it
    seemed.
But this "stuff" was not some invention of some byproduct
    sales scheme,
No.
This was the real stuff, the Earth's 'head cheese,'
Forged millions upon millions of years ago deep
    underground.
Cavalcades of crystalline cobbles,
Melted into some swirling superhot swill of molten magma,
Baked for 2.5 million years at 3600 degrees,
Crisped until a golden yellow brown,
Droozled with a rich layer of chocolatey charnockite,
Flecked with buttery biotite,
Rimmed by rich rhyolite,
With a hint of hematite,
A panache of pegmatite,
A splash of syenite,
And a dash of diorite,

All brainy bits of biospheric bones ground to breadbox bites
    for the trees to swallow,
Only to be extracted by some great, glacial floss one long-
    ago day,
Who knows what's in there anyway?

This 'tongue-twister' tale was inspired by an encounter with large chunks of rocks that appeared to have been blended by some giant cookie mixer, with bits of various rock types perfectly preserved in a matrix of granite. All types of rock were visible in this "conglomerate" in spite of the fact that it was igneous in origin and not settled out in some deep Cretaceous sea bed of sedimentation. I was surprised by the size of the embedded bits, as small as a half inch to over six inches in length. As an 'armchair geologist' I could not help but think about how this rock came about, and why it ended up in a pile on the side of the trail I was walking on. The colors were no less curious – pinks and reds, blues and purples, gray-brown to yellow-brown, all within a 'country rock' of rusty brownish yellow. It all reminded me of head cheese, as described above and now (fortunately) having mostly faded from my memory. I likened the rock to an equally odd type of creation!

Rick Van de Poll, Ph.D.

Emergence

I believe it was on a Thursday this year.
I awoke to that smell,
That ancient smell,
That all too familiar, how could I have forgotten it smell,
Faint at first, and then stronger,
Like that feeling of the days getting longer,
Or how lightening gives birth to thunder,
Inevitable.
Irresistible.
Irreversible.
Sap flowing, bud bursting, bark cracking symphonies
Loosening the lilt of lichenous litanies,
Everywhere
Heralding the coming on fragrant air,
At last,
Winter's grip receding,
Lost,
All evils of the world's bleeding,
Tossed,
Singed by crocus fire,
Unhinged by jonquil attire,
The recalcitrant recluse now dances and sings, the
Naked,
Pulsing,
Eruption of Spring!

There is that unmistakable moment, or perhaps a few, when the long winter days ultimately give up their grip on darkness and cold. For me it has always been more of a smell on the air, than any particular vista or sound. The daffodils and crocuses are fine, the return of birdsong is welcomed, yet the smell of sap flowing through the twigs of spring is like an ancient calling to life anew. This was how it was on my morning walk this day. I recalled thinking, Spring is, for most of life, a bountiful time, an arousal of the senses, a call for progeny to be created and passed on. It is neither good nor bad in the quickening of the senses, it is only elemental and right. Although Spring verdure speaks volumes of the passing of time, it is over all too soon, and quickly forgotten in all the fullness and bounty of summer.

Earth Day

Earth Day Earth Day
We go our own way,
Yet stop to pause,
On talons and claws,
And the breath and water that binds us.

For some it's a Holy Day
A day when we pray,
A blessing, a cause,
A sacramental pause,
The blood and the flesh that finds us.

Earth Conscious Day
Let's recycle they say,
And follow the laws,
While the pocket mouse gnaws,
Unaware, uncaring, and oblivious.

Just Another Day
It appears to be that way,
For the hoots, cackles and caws,
Hooves, hackles, and paws,
That remind us, are we really making a difference?

Live Life Fully Day
It should be that way,
No signs, marches, or mirages,

Nor speeches, crowds or applauses,
Just living every day like the whole world was watching
Every action
Every movement,
Every thought.

On this 47th Earth Day, I celebrated with a number of other 'believers' – i.e. those that think that Earth Day is *not* a sham, and that we owe it to our 'Great Sustainer' to honor that from whence we came. The fair I attended and presented at had a variety of visitors, from those who casually attend these things out of guilt or conscience or something akin to passive naïveté, to those ardent followers who strive to live life every day in honor of the "Mother." I fall somewhere in between those two extremes, perhaps trending towards the latter, yet still drive a car, live on the 'grid,' and support the generalized capitalist economy of which I am indelibly a part. That said, I recognize that life is an <u>opportunity</u> to be of service for the people, for the planet and for all wild things, and that to ignore this path can, perhaps, hasten one's own destruction. I also recognize that this path is not for most people; in fact, I find that it is, somewhat surprisingly, for but a very few individuals who are alive today.

The Vernal Pool

Lifeless, frozen pond
So cold I sit upon,
Ancient animals murmuring.
Waiting to be free
In some left-over sea,
That meltwater now is furthering.
Awaken thy spring!
Let life begin!
To the vernal voices, a gathering.
All peepers and frogs,
Hibernacu-logs,
Filled with the force of their fathering.
Time for abundance,
Unstoppable redundance,
In tune with Darwinian survivaling.
A vernal pool's charge
Is to grow things large
In the blink of a newt eye's revivaling.
One false step can change the very essence of evolution.

A slow slog through vernal pool mud inspired me to write this poem. The south edge was frozen solid but the north edge was open meltwater. What amazed me was the fact that life was already stirring awake during this later winter jaunt. And, that the life I witnessed had been cycling through this pool for countless generations across the ages. In a matter of days – or perhaps weeks during this cool wet spring, all manner of frogs and peepers and salamanders would be arriving from the winter hibernacula nearby – from beneath logs, leaf litter, and rock piles, to cascade into the pool during a night-time's rush of rain and warm temperatures. This process had been going on for millennia, and had developed life so specialized that if vernal pools not present on the landscape anymore, these species would not survive. It struck me that the footprints I was making in the mud was likely causing a subtle shift in the chemistry and food web in the water, and that I was therefore bringing about a possible change in the evolutionary pressures that had caused these organisms to adapt to a very tight niche.

Fairy Shrimp

Diminutive denizens of the deep,
On Midsummer's Eve in drought and heat,
That's when I cast,
My looking glass,
Upon the pond in which you sleep.

Belly down, along I creep,
Crunching brown the muddy seep,
How can you last,
Through years gone past,
Then spring to life aft summer's weep?

By fall you've grown an inch or more,
Settling in for your winter's store,
Of scum and slime, you'll eat no more,
Til spring unbinds and unwinds you.

Wide-eyed and pink, you'll take that drink,
Of vernal wine so clear,
Your home the size of a bathroom sink,
No matter, you find it dear.

Up close you're shod with phyllopods
Ten rows methinks I see,
Tail flaps your tiny cercopods,
You've spelled my reverie.

This poem was inspired by a walk through a vernal pool teaming with fairy shrimp. Although these inch-long creatures are not uncommon in the vernal pools of New England, there is always an odd 'mind-shift' that I undergo when seeing them with salamanders and frogs so far from the coast. Over twenty million years ago they say that coastal crustacea moved inland having adapted to freshwater systems. By then the climate had become favorable for adaptations that would lead them to becoming entirely reliant on a very short period of inundation in order to grow, breed and lay eggs. These 'BB'-sized eggs can lay dormant in pond muck for several years before emerging as larvae after a suitable combination of water and chemicals have eroded their tough outer casing. After emergence these ten-legged larvae go through several molts in a matter of a few weeks before developing egg and sperm sacs that allow them to reproduce and repeat the cycle again. Fascinatingly intricate, these tiny *Eubranchipus* are more compressed than seafaring shrimp but contain the same large eyes and ten sets of legs and breathing appendages that all shrimp contain.

Ancient Paths

Yesterday I took a walk,
Not just any kind of walk,
But a walk through time replete.
I lurched upon the moment
When
They took me down a road to then,
Smooth footfalls beneath my feet.
I cast a look to hinterlands,
Never expecting to meet
My ancestors
When
They took me down a road to then,
Campfire smoke and meat.
The spot was pleasant, a gracious lair,
Of bone and point and heat,
I settled in to tarry there,
When
They took me down a road to then.
'Neath mounds of dirt and root and snare,
And fenced-in stock so neat,
Sat piles of charcoal and dusty fare,
An excavator's treat,
When
They took me down a road to then.
They took me in to greet,
The passing of another age,
Re-living an ancient seat.

I was inspired to write this poem after discovering an aboriginal camp site along the Connecticut River. Having done this before, I was attuned to the likelihood of an encampment by virtue of the topography and proximity to hunting and fishing grounds. A soil auger was the tool I used to confirm the presence of several charcoal-laden fire pits on a low mound above the river. The depth of the charcoal, the mix of old wood ash and soil, and staining beneath the fire bed suggested a fairly long period of occupation. Sitting a while against a tree, I tried to imagine the flow of people on the spot, as well as what they did each day. Given the two hundred-fifty year absence of native peoples at this locale, it was not surprising that it was difficult to visualize, especially since such little evidence remains.

A Sad Rain

Southern wind
An Appalachian hymn
Of coal and stream and sadness,
Came wafting today,
A New England way,
To drench the misty madness.

Oft I fear
What I hold so dear,
Gone and lost the wildness,
Wet skin a quiver,
Not even a shiver,
Can warm the summer's shyness.

Oh when will it come,
That heart-warming sun,
To bring some sensibility,
To keep us safe,
And replace the rape,
Of mountaintop nobility.

For my part still,
I will warm my sill,
With wood and sweat and stillness,
And leave behind,
Those ruinous mines,
Which spread a drafty illness.

This poem was wrought by the winds from the southwest, which carried with them the air of mountaintop coal mining in West Virginia. Even in New England I could smell the stench of blasting coal and rock, of buried forests in the stream valleys of the Appalachians. Having seen this travesty once, I could not imagine what it would be like to wake up one day and see trucks removing the hill behind my home, while knowing that it will forever (or at least until the next ice age) bear the scar of human greed and short-sightedness. Burning coal for electricity is a nineteenth century solution to our own myopic needs, if not a hold-over from centuries before. To pollute the air with acid rain-causing chemicals that then drench my woods with sickness and starvation – (try absorbing water when you're loaded with sulfides and nitrates) – is a crime that no single species should endure. The foul air this day not only spoke of a cold, dark sadness that coal country must bear, it also epitomized the winter of our consciousness, where a more forgiving and creative spring seemed so far away.

Wood Pile Serenade

Would I to sing to my pile,
My lost and forlorn wood pile –
Its spring and I'm free,
And my pile is desperately
Gathering dust
And debris.
No worries I say, there will come another day
When flames lick bark,
And drive a new spark,
All bits of energy
Warming the frost of winter's gloss.
I rather delight in the time
To sit and stare,
Once stacked cordwood was sitting there,
No worries I say, there will come another day
Of growing trees in the sun,
Fiber and fuel,
Hauled this way and that,
Chasing away the nightmares
Of a February's fool.
Not I,
Not this winter,
Not this year,
My wood is still piled deep.
Here you must lay,
No worries I say, there will come another day
And I sing my pile to sleep.

This fanciful poem was inspired by yet another daily look at my dwindling wood pile. Today, however, it felt like winter was finally losing its icy grip. It was only a six-log day instead of a 10 or 12-log day. Hours upon hours of bucking and splitting later, I could now sit and relax next to what appeared to be a successful effort – here I was nearing the end of April and it was clear that I was *not* going to run out of wood this year. Having played this game for over 40 years now, it might seem that I would never have to face such a reality, yet not but a few years earlier, after an unseasonably cold and harsh winter, I actually ran out after having put away an extra three cord. Then there was the spring that never came when I was burning wood twice as fast in May as I did in April. And the time the snow hit the ground in early November and never relinquished itself until May. But these are merely New England tales of woe that we tell ourselves to keep from going stir-crazy on those dark, cold days, which, after all, are ones we choose to live!

Climate Change

Sweat pouring off our chins
Aft the rising to 410
We gather in crowds
To begin
The March
Towards our own self-induced destruction.
There is no basis they say
On this 80-degree April day,
That the climate is getting hotter,
Keep burning, why bother?
Just ride that Russian Trawler,
To the North Pole and farther,
"There is no basis I say!"
Throw a snowball in Congress,
Drill more, recycle less,
'Til the trout have all fried,
And the moose have all died,
And we're all forced to live inside.
Consider the options:
Act now, unite, speak out, and raise hope,
Or ride the slippery slope of lies, deceit, and destruction.
Reduce, reuse, and recycle
Or send your trash to the moon on a golden spoon.
Covet the sun, cherish the water, pray for the earth,
Or watch the children slowly die of disease, malnutrition,
     toxic shock, and overdose.
It is NOW we must choose,
There is no time to lose!

This poem followed a nationwide climate march I attended that involved millions and millions of people around the country. It was particularly poignant that on this day it was well over 80 degrees in New England and it wasn't even May. During this single yet impressive reminder of the effects that we as humans are having upon the Earth, it was outstandingly obvious that it is time for us to wake up as a species, as a people, and consider the cumulative effects were are having on the remainder of life on the planet. Despite the naysayers and fact debunkers there are some obvious truths that cannot be denied: that CO_2 is higher than it has been in several hundred thousand years, that average global temperatures have been higher in the last decade than ever before measured, and that storm frequency and severity have increased since the time we started paying attention to these things. The fall-out is beginning to show up, as so many of us have forewarned. Doesn't it seem odd that climate change deniers are accelerating their own destruction by their actions of ignorance and neglect? Having studied the history of our civilization, it can be said that this should not come as any surprise.

A Cedar's Tale

I arrived on the wind
A thousand
And a thousand years ago
(Or was it ten?)
It must have been,
Then,
On coastal air
I sank my roots deep,
In cold glacial fare,
Wet feet,
Just as I like it,
Deep peat,
All the better there.
 I was not alone back then,
Came butterfly my friend,
Who helped me find
Others of my kind,
A community to make,
An ecosystem to mend.
Unfurling my dark green cloak,
I shudder in fire and smoke,
Yet awake am I to those who listen,
Who breathe me in, searching high among limb,
Wearing mossy shoes in their two-by-two's,
Softly falling the light upon my leader,
I give to those of you the story of White-Cedar!

This poem followed a late spring trip to a cedar bog in the region at a time when ice was still upon the surface and walking was afforded across an untrammeled forest. The ancient, dark green boles and boughs were impressive enough, without having to remember that these were remnants from a old coastal environment, having pushed their way inland only a few thousand years ago during a time of a warming climate and sub-temperate conditions. Black gum, witch-hazel, beech, and oak arrived at that time as well, and with the help of Hessel's hairstreak butterflies, populated an otherwise cool temperate and boreal landscape with Atlantic White-cedar. Cedars were special, however, for they brought remarkable uses for the native peoples, not unlike those of the Big Cedar lands out west. Boxes, arrow shafts, fabric strips, and oil, the cedar was as versatile as it was forgiving. Relatively few stands remain, and fewer still are in pristine condition like the one I walked through this day.

A Great Weight

A great weight has been lifted today
From the highest of peaks
To the Rivers that Run —
A Return
Of the Sun
Has released the wrappings of winter's cloak,
All melting
Down
Like dripping candle wax
No sound,
Slipping
Beneath
The surface
We drown in the fragrance of thirsty bark,
All mossy and dark
Casting
Away
The shuddering fear
That holds us near the edge
Of unimaginable loneliness,
The aching cry of loon in wilderness
Deep
Asleep
Before the dawning of the day.

This poem came about from a pre-dawn rising and walk through warm winds in the forest. Loons nearby were back calling again on the pond for the first time this spring. The odor of wet twigs was strong upon the air, reminding me of early sap season when fresh fluids are splitting bark and bud in the mid-day sun. The snow was melting quickly now everywhere, with only patches left here and there in the woods. With the warming of the day I could imagine the earth subtly rebounding after being packed down with twelve feet of snow over the course of the winter. Water was running everywhere, on the surface of leaves, in small rivulets, along ditches, and down through the soil. For the first time in nearly two years, all of the pools and ponds were at full elevation from snowmelt and rain.

Lichen it or Not

Crispy curls on tender green furls
Where did you get your spiking?
From supernova swirls to watery worlds,
You must belong to lichen.

Those tiny green cells you hide so well,
Revealed on misty mornings,
No April's fool you totally rule,
The wake of winter's mourning.

Of stick and stone, bark and bone,
You creep and crawl without flaking,
A merry lot—you're not alone,
A fungus is part of your making.

Though spores be spread you look kind of dead,
All dry and brittle and baking,
 The summer's sun cannot be fun,
When no water's there for the taking.

Oh welcome fall rain, bring moisture again,
For twig and tripe and the trickling,
Of cortical cascades and stony palisades,
Awash with umbilical tickling.

British soldiers rise up and carry your red cup,
Apothecial salute to the dawning,
Lungwort sway down, your cephalodial crown,
Make food for the deer and their fawning.

Goatsbeard make rough the bristly tufts,
On pine and spruce and their branching,
Find veery and thrush and their ethereal hush,
Making nests of your weave and your lashing.

Yet its reindeer I pick making forests so thick,
That cloak ledge at its edge thus revealing,
That our age old home would be barren as bone,
Without lichenous licks for its healing.

This poem was inspired by walking through a bed of Cladonia (Cladina) lichen, otherwise known as 'reindeer moss.' Not a moss at all, these fascinating creatures are everywhere on the planet, all 38,000 species strong, from the edge of the sea to the highest of alpine zones. Lichens are exceptionally hardy, having withstood desiccating droughts and ultraviolet scorching for millions of years. Typically known as pioneers, they are actually present in all stages of forest and non-forest development, with some of them only appearing after the land has attained a great age. They help break down rock, soil, and organic matter, and are commonly responsible for much of the nitrogen uptake by plants in certain regions. My walk today was through a "forest" of 60-year old lichens that had reached their 'adulthood' at three inches in height!

The Last Mastodon

Tree trunk legs standing knee deep in mud,
Ears twitching always alert,
The dark glossy coat shines
Even in the late twilight.
Laborious lips lick
A tasty slick.
The patient sway,
A settling in,
Speaks volumes of
Timeless kin.
Ancient long-haired ones
Remember
A distant time
Longing to begin,
A quicker beast
A little more trim,
A proboscis now more sublime.
Twig-eaters at a muddy bar,
Order up spritzers
Of birch and bark,
The heart-shaped hooves
No longer tar-tainted dark.
Yet carry on they must
All the while looking back,
A cavalcade of memories
Of their evolutionary track.
Of camels and saber-tooths
And wolves that were dire,

Came long spears and clovis points,
Meat sizzling over fire.
Now vehicles and guns,
At a much faster clip,
Belie time and survival
This is no Darwinian trick,
Instead, global warming
Brings on winter tick,
So moose must move on,
A branch tip affair
For the last mastodon
Is losing its final lair.

This ode to one of our most noble animals in New England was brought on by the sighting of yet another moose affected by winter tick in our neighborhood. The paltry color and irregular blotching were the telltale signs. This one sat still, quite still in fact, sopping up salt-laden mud in the front yard. He was in no hurry, velvety antlers still pumping blood, as he slurped up a tasty slurry of roots and soil. This one had been here before, for two years in fact, coming to the same seep in early May just off the roadway where tasty licks remained after a winter's worth of snow salt use. Unfortunately for him, the concomitant increase in salt use has gone along with the increase in icy roads, which in turn have arisen from warmer winter temperatures that have made the roads slicker and winter ticks fatter on his skin. I fear for these last bastions of large herbivores in our midst, regardless of where their ancestry is from, which, fancifully posed, reminded me of how mastodons were eliminated from the Earth at the hands of man.

Spring Color

Shhhh it's a secret!
The northern hills aflame?
Must be September
As long as I can remember,
Tour buses and fairs,
School sales and cider mills,
And bears fattening up for winter –
But no!
Tis spring instead,
Trees wakening from the dead,
Flowering maples fill the dawn
Like so many trinkets on a Christmas lawn, swaying
In a gentle breeze
Promises of summer
A hopeful air,
And there,
Creeping up the slopes of time
A riotous chorus of green –
Kelly green
Grayish green
Sea-breeze green
Melodious green
Verdant green
Unstoppable, yet ephemeral
All too soon awash in forest green,
All equal, 'vanilla fudge' indiscernible,
Fluttering gaily in the wind

Like so many mosquitoes that keep the head down not
  noticing such things anyway.

This poem was brought about by a view across the valley on an early spring day. The colors were wrought in all shades of leaf-emerging green, that varied by species, hillside, and elevation. It was a remarkable sight, that mostly goes unnoticed – the aspens that silver up so early, the red maples that dash the hillsides with pink, the sugar maples that scatter here and there in a bright yellow-green, the beeches that make kelly green look pale, and the ashes that still look dead on the stump. For those of us waiting through long gray winters, this splash of spring finery is not to be missed, no matter what the fall foliage enthusiasts say!

Tree Ring Story

Tree ring count in a cedar swamp,
Guesses all around – 130? 150? 180? Or more?
Imagine its age,
It's all in the core.
Older than the adjacent development,
Older than that nearby street,
Older than the last world war,
Imagine its age,
It's all in the core.
What about the Depression,
Or Dust Bowl
Or Great War?
Imagine its age,
It's all in the core.
How about the Gay Nineties,
Or Spiritualists
Or Civil War?
Imagine its age,
It's all in the core.
Then maybe the Golden Spike
The Erie Canal
Or 1812 war?
Imagine its age,
It's all in the core.
Perhaps the birth of a nation
The Revolution,
'Ere seven years and four score,
Imagine its age,

It's all in the core.
A count to the center
Exceeded all that,
Forty-five presidents
And colonial spat.
This tree graced the land
A seedling at best,
When Mic-Mac
And Abenaki
Sat down to rest,
Against ancient ones
That cast seed
After four hundred years or less,
In a swamp tucked away,
Now lost in folklore,
Imagine an age,
It's all in the core.

This poem arose from a day-long workshop I taught on wetland evaluation techniques in a well-known Atlantic white-cedar swamp. After the discussing the perfunctory role of wetlands in creating such swamps, and the innumerable functions they serve to improve society, we paused a moment to admire the old growth cedar trees. They were magnificent. At the suggestion of one member, I pulled out my tree corer and tested a venerable bole. Taking it back out was not easy trick as the rings were so tight they appeared to be under pressure to expand and fluff away. A carefully inserted straw helped that out, whereupon I brought it back, dried it, mounted it on a core mount board, and smoothed it to a fine grain surface. Three hundred and fifty years of counting from a core three feet off the ground!

Wilderness Lost

At what point did we lose wilderness?
When wildness turned to kindredness,
When flags were placed on Everest,
When space became a race,
Lunar modules creasing the Old Man's face,
When the Titanic hit the ocean floor,
Only to become a great movie score,
When the 'War to End All Wars'
Became just another story,
A miserable tale of aggression and glory,
When subtlety turned to sublimity,
And wonder lived no more,
Write me a new dictionary,
Cast out the words we abhor!
Like carrot
Or poppy
Or camping
Or boar,
Make me sit up and listen some more.
Oh wildness can you speak to me, tell me why or wherefore?
You know I cannot just live caged up indoors,
I long for wild places,
No roof, wall, or floor,
Where no man has been,
Forever more! Forever more!

This poem came about after walking in a driving rain that temporarily cast out any thought of all but the weather and my immediate surroundings of unbridled woods. I had been out hiking in a vast tract of unfragmented land earlier in the week, and it struck me that even while doing that, I came across the signs of a culture now long gone – the agricultural era of 19th century New England. The age of the woods like the driving rain, provided an illusion of wildness, of untrammeled nature, and yet I knew this was not true. In fact, after some contemplation, I could not imagine a place on Earth anymore that was free from the signs, smells, and sounds of human activity. While there are some vast stretches of wildness left, it appears that these places are getting smaller and smaller every year, regardless of whatever legal protections they have placed upon them.

Black-throated Green Warbler

Silent, then
Tentative at first,
Perhaps waiting
For the right time to burst
Into your song
"See-see-see-you'll-see."
I wonder how the winter went,
In tropical palms and sand
A far cry from snowy trees bent,
Nice to leave a frozen land.
How did you make it this far?
Through storms and wind and rising tides,
Never a chance to stop or glide,
Across the sea you carried on,
A two ounce mini marathon,
More feather than skin,
You begin again, gleaning
Your call from the treetops
You have me leaning far over
My thoughts – "You're late!"
Your kin's already here,
Insect lunch is on the plate
Spring is in full gear,
"Why take time to come so near (to me)?"
See-see-see-you'll-see.

This light-hearted poem was inspired by one of my favorite songsters of spring, the Black-throated Green Warbler. Aside from the fact that it is a tiny might of a bird that typically resides high in the treetops away from view, it beckons the onset of early spring and is therefore a welcome addition to the rising chorus of birds in the wood. By numbers, this bird has always been plentiful, hence as a child I was able to hone in on its song and learn it well. The occasional male will drop down and grace a person with a good solid look, even daring to be closer in proximity than most warblers. The young are equally as curious, as if they need to learn who it is that is making all that racket nearby. The gleaners like these always receive my utmost respect, for what would our woods be without these insect-eating, bright and colorful songsters to keep company with?

A Winter Wind

A cold wind came down from the North today,
A Winter wind,
A reminder of what has been, of wood piles, thick socks, and
    icy mountaintops
On this seventh day of May.
I caught myself in a shudder,
And turned to face the intruder,
A cold, cheek-blushing, nose-dripping stare
As if to say,
This is not what I bargained for,
All shadowed, cold, and gray.
But this wishful thinking warmed me not
Nor lightened the indulgence upon my sorry lot –
No!
Instead, I must endure,
Look forward, onward and away,
For tulips turn the tide of spring
And melt despair away.
'Tis but winter's duel with solar fuel
That racks the trees at hand,
It has no chance of relinquishing the dance
Of greening up the land.
I'm reminded of this inevitable way,
No need then for any dismay,
The winds will come and go,
And Winter's death, like Spring's final breath,
Will wither ice and snow.

Living in New England comes with a few pluses and minuses, but mostly just weather. Just when things are warming up, a cold winter wind blows hard upon the day just as it did this day. I've seen heavy snow this late in the year, so I suppose a bit of cold, icy wind was not so bad. Yet in contrast to the first coat-stripping, sun-blazing days of early spring, these 'regressions' are sometimes hard to take. On this day the north wind was racking the trees as if it were January, with no thought whatsoever about the fact that in a mere two weeks the land would be green once again.

The Great Unfurling

I believe it begins in late winter,
That silent messaging among the roots,
Molecule by molecule,
Driven by an unknowable truth, a belief, really, that the day
　　will come,
And again,
And again,
Warmer still beneath the sill of ice and snow,
Silent messaging, telling the truth known only to fern,
The great unfurling has just begun.
Slowly at first, to the eye imperceptible,
But to the meristem incontrovertible,
An arising, like so many things in spring,
A call to ancient voices that no longer sing.
Gaining strength, cracking pavement, pushing logs and
　　smashing crust,
A fiddlehead bears a million year trust
Of emergence,
Of resurgence,
Beyond the caves of man,
Beyond all dinosaur land,
So formidable, so predictable, the greenery capturing shade
　　every day,
Yet delicate and soft, feathery aloft, this pterophyte
Breaking brakes,
Gathering gates,
Of light and limb and wonder

This night,
Every night,
Exposing the simplicity of life unfurled, untouched, asunder.

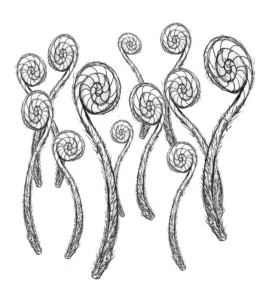

This poem was inspired by the witnessing of an unfurling fiddlehead in the woods behind my house. It fact, there were several hundred of them – tall ones, skinny ones, solitary ones, all different shades of green, some cloaked in a fuzzy down, others bearing scales, other naked in the morning sun. I thought about this while driving around on fern compost soup – oil, that is, which has spanned beyond anyone's imagination of time. So fantastic to know that ferns in and of themselves have survived that long on Earth. Albeit they were a bit larger in the Cretaceous – up to a hundred times larger than they are now for some, they were nonetheless ferns with all of their parts and their great unfurling in spring long before fiddles were even invented.

Two Bears Came Running By

Two bears came running by,
One a little bold, the other a little shy.
They reminded me of myself
During days now long gone by—
Running through the woods carefree,
No thought to slow me down,
Agile and more nimble then,
Sniffing all around.
They appeared of a sudden all black then gray then black
    again,
As they dodged behind trees,
A bouldery beech woods had drawn them in,
Grubbing nuts beneath the leaves.
The first one, slightly larger with ears tucked back,
A rippling mass of muscle and black,
Came zipping by within feet of my gaze,
Nose to the ground, completely unfazed.
The second, smaller, all about giving chase,
With huffs and growls and an impressive pace,
Caught wind of my scent and gave up the race,
Nose to the air, caught sight of me standing there,
A few yards away, a huge smile on my face.
Man looked at Bear, and Bear looked at Man,
And across that great span
Of time – seconds, minutes, perhaps a millennium –
There dawned that look –
That 'oh-my-god-what-am-I-doing-here' sort of look,

That 'I-believe-I-bumbled-into-danger' sort of look,
And that 'Now-what-do-I-do' sort of look.
Yet curious bear, with patience still,
Tested my resolve to stand stock still.
A step towards me, and then another,
My mind praying to my four-legged brother:
"Care not, tarry not, my species deserves little affection,
Because bear heads on walls are but a minor confection,
Your land is what we want, all the trees and all the stones,
To build monuments to ourselves, heaped upon ancestral
    bones
To applaud how smart we are
To tell the world we are king
The human race dangling on a string,
Alone,
All greedy,
Narcissistic and needy,
No, tarry not my brother in this traveling wood,
Your curiosity is a death knell in this human neighborhood."
"Take your sister and run as far as you can,
Better to play on a distant star than give chase on this land,
For we bipeds lack foresight and care not for your kind,
Another distraction, another predator, another animal to
    bind,
And cast away save gall bladders and such,
If you want to live I can tell you this much,
Shyness is a virtue, four legs and a nose,
For then we can't hurt you or keep you enclosed,
So run now my brother, go tell all the others,
To keep distance, stay away,
Perhaps one day
You will lose the stench of us, for thee I will pray."

Rick Van de Poll, Ph.D. • 61

This poem came about by virtue of a direct encounter in the deep woods of two bears. As I was walking quietly, the raucous thrashing of two adolescent bears chasing each other allowed me to remain effectively hidden even though I was in plain sight. The first bear ran by me within a few feet of where I stood and didn't take any notice of my whereabouts. The second bear only came about after detecting my scent while slowing his chase across boulders and between trees. It was at that moment, at about thirty feet away, that he saw me standing there watching him. The look on his face was priceless, especially how it changed from 'whoa' to 'uh-oh' to 'oh crap.' After that split second realization with me standing completely still, we shared a few "thoughts" as we stared into each other's eyes. A couple of steps closer and he had apparently had enough of the non-verbal communication and turned and walked calmly away.

The Mystique of Morels

Of all of God's creations, there is none like the morel.
Tall and stately, at least to a slug,
It rises from the earth, all golden and smug.
And well be its claim from such a lowly plug
Of earth and root in a cellar hole once dug,
For thou art the Queen court jesters do tell,
The mystical, magical, mighty morel!
I've searched 'cross miles of hill, dale and dell,
Only to come up empty-handed, no mushrooms to sell,
Aft' fields of rumors too easy to quell,
Not a one came today to drop in my pale.
Oh golden wonder what secrets you keep,
Decades between fruiting erst while you sleep deep,
I dream of you piled high in a mountainous heap,
Only then will I claim a true bounty to reap,
And settle at last the score that I keep.
Twenty-and-one trips to this memorable spot
Where I found you once alone all naked and hot,
In the sun,
Reeling me in, like a crab to a pot,
Then scalded and burned, my hopes left to rot,
Nary a sign since then, you're such a paltry lot,
Dashed dreams, old visions is all that you've brought,
To teach patience to me, a perseverating sot,
And wisdom to know that the morel of the story
Is that you can never be bought with fame nor glory!

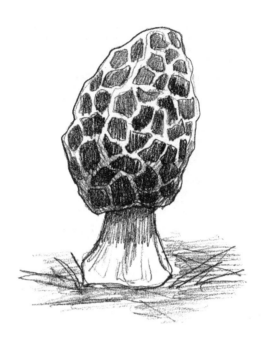

On this day I made my annual pilgrimage to the only somewhat reliable morel spot near my home, and prayed once again for good luck. After a phenomenal spring full of rain, I thought, this was going to be the year. But alas, my prayers were perhaps not sincere enough, for while I did find a morel – a large one at that – it was but old, withered and bleached by the sun. Out of deference to the morel Gods (are you listening?) I left it in place. Long have I wondered about the mysteriousness of morels, a member of a mysterious kingdom. I've recounted tales of a twenty year absence from a single yard, and of dozens of fruit bodies in one year at a single spot and none ever again. Those of us "in the know" pretend we can predict where and when they occur, but here in the East, we are but fools to think we have 'cracked the code' of the mighty morel!

Greening of the Earth

No Emperor, no plebian, no knave, King or Queen,
Can give me the stature I get from the Green,
No religion, no doctrine, no spirit unseen,
Can give me the faith I get from the Green,
Even pink people, teal people or those in between,
Can give me the color I get from the Green,
For Green is the color of life I have seen,
A blessed color, a vibrant color, a water drop's dream,
The Earth's rising up, from whence I have been,
Exciting my senses, inviting me in,
To eat wild, run naked, and jump in a stream,
Roast skunk cabbage, chew dandelion, shun helleborine,
Brew coltsfoot, steep yarrow, make powerful medicine,
Engage plant spirits and animal spirits to heal me within,
Plant seeds, breathe deep, bring life back again.

This poem was inspired by the remarkable spring greens that were everywhere upon the land at this juncture of the season. From bleak barren brown and ghostly gray, the emergence of spring greenery has long fascinated me both scientifically and artistically. At an early age I became enamored with the greening of the Earth in spring – while some children were playing with guns and telling stories of make-believe war, I was illustrating leaves and pressing plants. Even after the world of wildlife opened up to me with backyard birds, fishing and hunting, the plant world continued to dominate my endeavors both as a past-time and as a profession. The Green World then became solidly my mentor and savior in times of need ever after.

Following the Path

Somewhere high in the sky it formed,
I'm not sure exactly where,
But upon my sleeve,
All sharp and glistening,
A droplet was sitting there.
I bent down, looked close,
And gave it a good stare,
Ten billion molecules have made it at once appear.
Cautiously, slowly, it drops to the ground,
And penetrates deep without a sound,
There it joins others, and even more there still,
Until and until, after roots have had their fill,
An underground stream forms, a portentous swill.
Seeps, springs, and sinkholes, and eventually a rill,
The roller-coaster ride begins, rushing downhill.
Which way will it go, this tiny drop of mine,
To mossy leaf, or brook trout's wine.
Perhaps it will miss these biotic affairs,
Miss water pipe, and beaver trap snares
And make it downstream to a giant waterfall,
Rushing, gushing, and amply tall,
To get airborne again,
Vaporized by all,
Struck by the sun
Lofted into cloud,
And rainbowed in my mind's eye from sleeve to the sky.

This was a rainy day in the field, with ample time to witness firsthand the presence of water in all forms. The droplet on my sleeve sparkled in the sun while it fell to Earth, and thereupon began an amazing journey I could only imagine. On the molecular level I could envision the possible path of such a droplet, from sky to aquifer to river or stream and then back again to sky. With an infinitude of possible pathways, this fanciful thought made me wonder where all of the water droplets in my body came from and to where they may eventually end up again.

Sitting on a Rock

Sitting on a Rock,
As life goes by,
I let the time grow thin,
I release my senses from keeping track
Of arms and legs and skin,
I relax into the age,
And wonder now
Where my sitting Rock has been,
From molten magma to sea bed sediments
And back to crystalline.
White, without shadow,
Bright even at sundown,
Molten quartz so long ago cooled,
My perfect seat has transcended this feat
And turned another page.
Glacial ice has moved me still,
Atop a pile of other till,
Coming back again and again and again, until
I looked down from the crest of a knobby hill,
Where weather carved a face on me,
And proclaimed me as a sage.
Trees grew up, pushing grasses back,
To let me rest in shade,
And mosses replaced the lichen cloak,
And softened my façade.
Then farmers came and cleared the land,
With sweat and stock and prayer

They said God made them do it that way,
To set stock upon the range.
Through wars and drought and living without,
The Farmers lost their way,
The sheep no longer bared my back,
Soon trees took center stage.
This time they fell to grinding tools,
That scraped and clawed and shook,
Replaced by towers of steel and line,
That gave me a brand new look.
My world's now bare, no forest there,
What grows is soon cut down,
A buzzing hums inside my ear,
From dusk until the dawn.
So sit my friend, and try to pretend,
What life once used to be,
Remember my seat, rest your traveling feet,
Let your thoughts of me run free.

This poem arose while sitting on a nice quartzite boulder at the edge of a powerline in Rindge. First and foremost it provided me with a place to rest after a long bushwhack through wetlands and forest. But while sitting there I tried to imagine what this rock had seen since it first formed deep within the Earth's crust hundreds of millions of years earlier. The passage of geologic time of course, dwarfs anything we as humans have known, and yet, it bears witness to relive this passage to the extent possible, if for no other reason than to put into perspective our very brief history upon the Earth.

A Warm Breeze

A warm breeze hit me hard today
Right across my face,
It had all the promise of summer winds created by the
    human race.
For truth be told I think it bold,
For people to own a place.
Perhaps it is a different tack to say that land ne'er gives back,
For back is not to give,
The land lives life unto itself,
And not for where we live.

This summer's breeze, all full of ease, has cast a spell on me,
To make it seem, as if in a dream, that choice is always free.
Yet the limits to growth is no small joke, for people, place,
    and Earth,
In our dying do we rarely find true value in our worth.
For who has cast upon a stone their writ of life in sum,
And tarried there in humble prayer, to serve our guardian
    home?

The wind blows hard and breaks a shard of dawning in my
    mind,
That Spring is nigh, aft Winter's sigh, and peace is hard to
    find.
We all must bear it, through seasons of merit, what works
    we leave behind,
And size ourselves up, in a champagne cup, to toast our
    humankind.

This poem speaks volumes about the dilemma of being of the Earth and yet, as a singular species, accelerating global climate change. The warm breeze I felt was filled with the air of the metropolis to the south, and carried with it an odor not unlike the smog I recalled from the 60's prior to the Clean Air Act. Having lived in Mexico City at a time when air quality was perilously dangerous to breathe (I was not alone in wearing a mask), I likened the air this day to a 'deja-vu' of times thankfully past. And yet, the unnatural warmth and odor cast a sickly spell upon the mountain slopes where I live. How long, I wondered, can we continue to burn fossil fuels and remain free of the fatal effects of 'unsequestering' millions of years or carbon? There are clearly no simple answers, only theories that vary according to politics and global design.

The First Baptism

I long for the season of water.
Before winter's lost its icy grip,
And tannin tea offers a tasty sip,
Comes the anticipation of a frigid dip,
In crystalline clear pure water.
Tis a ritual for me,
Shedding clothes, feeling free,
Plunging in the open sea.
No matter if the weather's hot,
Or rainy cold, it matters not,
For once submerged, I lose all thought,
Of what it's supposed to be.
In fact there is no better way,
To drive the winter's woes away,
To greet the fullness of the day,
In lake or pond or stream.
I liken the act to a sacred pact,
Between sun and moon and starry black,
Regaining the light that winter's lacked,
So we can joyfully be.
It's coming soon to a pool near you,
That chance to sharpen your senses too,
To take the dive and become alive,
And breathe baptismally.

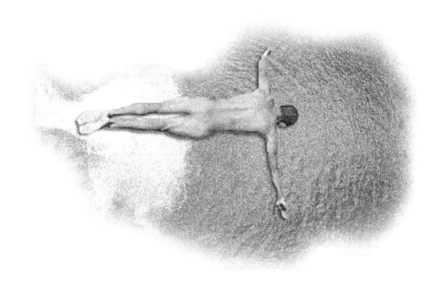

This day was the day of my first "polar plunge" in a mountain stream nearby. I believe snow had just fallen on the mountaintops, or so it seemed as this act simply took my breath away. I don't exactly remember the first time I did this as a child, but age seven or eight comes to mind. With some encouragement in college, I learned the fine art of 'sauna snow swimming' whereupon the necessary ingredients were both hot *and* cold. Since then, the 'hot' has been a good hard run, hiking up a mountain, or simply basking in an unusually hot sun prior to immersion. Ritualistically I have adopted the spring 'plunge' to honor the flow of fresh water and the release of winter's icy grip upon the land.

Incoming Storm

They were mere wisps at first,
A lazy drift across the open sky,
The filling in between the lines
A watercolor pie;
Then slowly came the massive round
O'er mountain tops of green,
Those wondrous mounds of lenticular clouds,
In sunset's hoary sheen.
Like feather down so soft and round,
The billows did belie,
A pillowed quilt was being bound
Across the sodden sky.
The wind came up as it always does,
With fury now impending,
Big fat drops in luscious gusts,
Promised sheets of rain unending.
A moment thus, the hillside hush,
Of bird and life awaiting,
That unspeakable silence before the rush,
I find is so elating.
For then the throng, a thunderous song
Drowns all who have been listening,
To drink from the sky the tears of Earth's eye,
And wash rainbows from the glistening.

This poem was inspired by the very first thunderstorm of spring after a brief but unforgettable 90-degree set of days in May. The storm arose in a classic way, and I was able to watch its development across the span of a couple hours as I completed some fieldwork nearby. Not unlike so many of the thunderstorms I have been caught out in, this one provided a welcome relief to the sweltering heat that my winter's body was not quite yet accustomed to!

La Chanson du Pissenlit

Les dents de Lion
Son vert et mordant,
Comme quelques chose de la vie,
Leur base principes
Qui son plus profonds
Pour mettre a terre authentique.
J'y vrai écrire une chanson,
A honorer le lion,
Duquel dents animé la plante effréné,
Et celebrer in vers, pour tous le monde a écouter
La puissance de cette herbe peu elevé.
Je connais les peoples qui peut étudier
Une chose ou deux sans regret,
S'affirmer avec esprit et determiné
Requerie ne frivole ni vous etrê.

<u>English Translation</u>

The teeth of the lion
Are green and bitter
Like so many things in life,
Their well-rooted base,
That's so very deep,
Grounds them well into the earth.
I'd really like to write a song,
To honor the lion,
Whose teeth inspired the wild plant,
And celebrate in verse, for all the world to listen to

The power of this lowly herb,
I know some people who would do well to study,
A thing or two without regret,
To affirm oneself with spirit and resolve,
Requires being neither superficial nor your (typical) self.

Upon teaching one of several edible and wild medicinal plant classes this year I found myself reflecting on the dandelion, a common plant that virtually every participant knew, but which very few had used or eaten. I also reflected on the origin of the name, with the lobes of the leaf looking like lion's teeth according to some enterprising soul who named it "dents de lion." I wondered how long ago this was, and if that person was at the time also using it for medicine to stimulate liver activity, relieve aches or pains, add Vitamin A to the diet, or even roasting the roots for a beverage. The scientific name, *Taraxacum officinale*, suggests that the plant was well known as a medicinal herb long before Carl von Linne's time in the mid-1700's when he dubbed this plant with its first Latin binomial. In honor of the 'continental' origin of the name I decided to have a try at a French poem by dusting off some long ago linguistics from a time when French was required in our schools!

The Veery and the Thrush

At the end of this day,
This perfect day of spring,
Came two birds into my yard,
Purposefully wandering.
One sang loud and clear and melodious,
The other, softer, sadder, a little tenuous.
Sang one "I'm from La Tuileries and thee?"
The other "Verily, verily, verily I see."
Both carried on indeterminably,
A melody cast so ethereally
I could not help but wonder,
Barring wind, rain, or thunder,
How could the world not listen
To the essence of thrush's mission.
Tho' quest I far across this land,
I cannot match with wit or hand,
The beauty of these paired refrains,
Ventriloqual, haunting, yet full of fame.
Thus the ringing of day's end's rung true,
For singing in woods and oft in plain view
Are the guardians of evening, thrush and veery too,
Singing lullabies to spring's life borne anew.

Clearly inspired by two thrushes in the evening, this poem reflects on the indescribable nature of bird song and how it can elicit feelings, thoughts, and memories that push the limits of our consciousness. Perhaps best known as the most cited favorite among birders, evening thrushes come in at least five forms and several dialects across North America. There are few forest areas where they do not live, and they can occur even in those non-forest deserts and scrublands that receive them in migration or in the winter.

Tree Story

Imagine
That leaves have grown and fallen
For one hundred lifetimes on a single tree
Spreading branches wide   slightly to one side
A merriment of light   captured   by every ray of the
sun
The perfection   of each   hands in
prayer held high
Wind always breathing   the tree   listening
Stories told of old   and old   and older
Than we can imagine   of times before leaves   were
written upon
Bark no longer useful   cooked instead for bread
The wars of men   so many
A gentle rain reminds
To never end
But begin
Again
And
Again
And
Again.

This 'poetry art' was inspired by the sighting of several old growth sugar maples in the midst of a deep wood. Each exceeded 300 years in age, and had therefore seen countless days, seasons, and the passing of culture on the land. Seedlings well before the American Revolution, these trees were already good sized poles by the time the first white settlers were clearing the forest for agriculture in the late 18th century. They had seen the woods around them spared likely for producing maple sap, and then witnessed not one but three great wars that took men away to war. They reminded me of a nine thousand year-old ebony tree that I admired one day in a woodworker's shop nearby, which had been passed down from king to king, pharaoh to pharaoh somewhere east of the Nile. That trees could live 'one hundred lifetimes' gave me pause about our passing human imprint upon this Earth.

Discrimination

It all happened in the midst of a field.
This was not any ordinary field, no –
This was a teaching field, a learning field,
A field of discrimination.

Have you ever tried to find a needle in a haystack, or in this
case, a single plant – a grass no less – in the middle of a
field?
I remember finding my car keys once in the middle of a vast
sandy beach, a mile and a half from where I'd lost them.
Then there was that glove in mid-winter, caught up on some
barbed wire, hours of bushwhacking earlier, impossibly
tucked up into the air.
Or my best friend in the middle of a coastal rainforest of
gigantic trees, lost for hours and hours, somehow
finding my daypack I'd left for him high in a tree where
I'd seen him last...
But this was a single plant, like every other plant, green,
invisible, slender.
My task? Locate it, identify, mark, and record.
Apparently, this was the last one of its kind in the state.
And so I began.
At first, every plant looked the same to me, all of those
grasses, all of those leaves,
Swaying gently in the breeze. Finally I stopped, bent down,
looked close –
I studied shape and hue, tuft and mound, blade and ligule,
each part absolutely miniscule,

Until, and just then,
A crack appeared in my blurry vision,
An opening in my mind perhaps, I could not tell, just a
    whisper I suppose –
They're all different!
Every
Single
One.
Every single life form had its own story to tell,
Each had its own size, its own companions, its own place in
    the dell,
And so I bent down very close now, opened up and asked
    again,
"Will you show me the way to my graminoid friend?"
And slowly, gently, they bent over and spoke,
"Come unto us with open mind,
Fear not to be a little blind,
For life is full of mystery,
That make us lose our history,
Cast aside both fact and truth,
Unmask the lies you learned in youth,
That all things great and all things small,
Must look alike after all."

Crawling on all fours,
I felt like a mouse as I navigated the stems as if they were
    trees.
The tunnels were caves with walls of dead leaves.
The ferns were like fortresses, fenceposts bent at the knees.
And there, just there,
Was my friend in a patch,
A remnant of aboriginal days, bare space between thatch,

Decumbent and rare, no other plant could quite match,
Vibrant and green, casting out seed for my nimble hands to
    catch.

Freed from the vision of everything same,
I welcomed the search in this Lilliputian game,
For truth dawned in leaf, in flower, and in fame,
That we live a myopic life, our blindness to blame.

This poem was inspired by a half-day search for *Paspalum setaceum*, the slender-leaved panic-grass in the midst of a wide meadow. At first it appeared that it was in impossible task, looking for a grass that was but a couple inches tall in a sea of grasses and forbs that stood well above the knee. But slowly, after locating a few clumps, I began to recognize the pattern in the hayfield, and learned how each small shift in slope, exposure, soil depth, and moisture created a myriad of microclimates that were at once discernable and predictable. It reminded me of how we often look at people, whether in a particular town, or particular state, of even a particular country and see only the commonalities that bind them together without really seeing them as individuals. Whereas many of us discriminate against "others," few of us take the time to discriminate individuals without bias or prejudice.

Copperhead Creed

If I do not exist, do you?

There was once a time when copperheads dined
On mice and moles and men,
Though Men it would seem, learned quickly to deem
That snakes are better off dead.

Shovels be damned, their tools of the killing,
Men driven by fear, all the while filling
Their predatory pockets with a ransomous shilling,
This was the Copperhead's creed, all blamed on God's
    willing.

'Twas the dominion of man, and not lowly snake
That led us to blame Eve for our very own mistake,
For knowledge wasn't evil, nor apple a drake,
Just a reminder of the guilt we feel when we take
All power, all life, all love for our own sake.

So let me give back the flag, snake tread on me please,
I deserve not to walk but crawl on my knees,
And learn humility and forgiveness, I beg of you please,
I will recast your symbol, and change the Copperhead
    Creed.

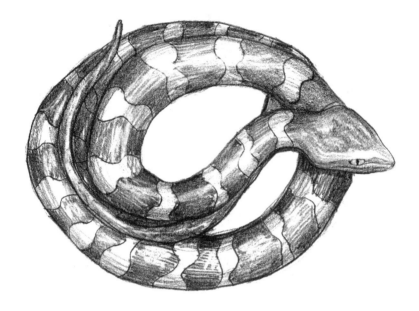

This poem arose upon the sight of a northern water snake, a harmless, non-venomous snake that is often killed by those who think it a copperhead and therefore poisonous. Copperheads were once common in central and southern New England, but were largely killed off for fear of being bitten by them. Although venomous, the last known poisoning from a copperhead was well before the 19th century. As a result we have scant few left today, and, like the eastern timber rattlesnake, they are barely hanging on in but a very few ancestral dens and haunts. The part about the shovel was added on account of my personal observation of such a snake killing, which took place when I was seven at the hands of my own grandfather, who I thought was otherwise a very reasonable man. The result: I have praised and revered water snakes ever since.

Achieving Yellow

Somewhere seeds are popping in the Kalahari desert sun,
Scattering
A perfect trajectory
Upon the Earth.
Glossy green leaves grow,
Emerging
From winter's slumber
On a maritime turf.
Dandelion's dangle at the edge of the cliff,
Sparkling
In the noonday sun
On a Scottish moor.
Lazy daisies droop their afternoon heads,
Dazzling
In fields of gold
On a Caucasian steppe.
The call of the yellow is strong in this world,
Rising
Ever rising
To greet the Father
To merge with the Creator
To become one with the sun.
Irresistibly, I crush cress flowers between my teeth and think
    of these things.

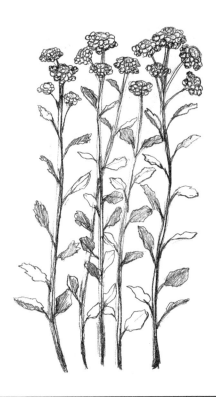

The inspiration for this poem was the emergence and welcome greeting of the first wintercress flowers of spring. More than any other flower in the Northeast, this has become an iconic symbol of rebirth and new beginnings, all of which are imparted in the very taste of this delicious potherb. I use cress as much as possible in soups and salads, sauces, and steamed vegetables, partly because of the wonderful yellow color they impart on all else cooked, and partly because of the exceptional mustardy taste. In good years, their season can last more than a month, and their ubiquitous occurrence ensures that this taste of spring lasts well into early summer.

Coast Coming In

Well, that's settled now.
Time to shutter in.
The Nor'east wind is blowing hard,
And rain is falling thin.
A coastal rain, all full of mist,
And fog and salt and tide,
I cannot help but think I'm there,
Sou'wester at my side.
For summer's promise is in the air,
Her warm breeze is on my face,
My lips can taste her salty fare,
My arms her warm embrace.
The surge of the sea I feel inside me,
Waves crashing at my feet,
Revealing the lure of a distant shore,
Of sirens yet to meet.
I wander there upon the air,
And dream Odyssean nights,
Of candlelight rituals and sumptuous victuals,
Plucked hardily from the bight,
Of ambrosian feasts and unending wine,
Debauchery until daylight,
Of the gentle rock of a swaying ship,
And dreams that end just right.
But mine is now a casual affair,
Walking my dog in twilight,
My coat is now soaked, my feet are sopping wet,
Clear skies are nowhere in sight.

I must then return, light fire and burn
The heat back into my bones,
Let the seaworthy mist carry on with its tryst,
Singing verses so far from my home.

Inspiring this poem was a thick misty rain that fell upon me at twilight while walking my dog one evening. The smell of the low clouds was nothing short of salty, as if the air had skipped the hundred or so miles from the sea and landed in my midst. The salty air and misty rain brought back many memories, some actual, some perhaps from lifetimes ago when the seafaring life was mine. I wanted to honor the power of scent and our olfactory sense in dredging up memories of distant lands and distant times.

Rick Van de Poll, Ph.D.

The Mystique of Morels II

Arising
Like a breath from the underground,
The mycelial mesh
Takes hold,
Grabbing onto root and mold,
Unfolding
It curls up, and up
Delicate cups
Scattering
Atop hollow madness
Bringing joy
And gladness
To those
Who witness
The miracle
Of mushroom life
Unfolding.

This poem was inspired by another uncommon occurrence of morel mushrooms in a friend's yard. Forty-eight of them to be exact. Somewhat of a surprise. In the East, such things are revered beyond most culinary delicacies from the wild, largely I suppose, on account of their rarity. We do not have such things as snowbank morels, or montane conifer morels, or post fireburn morels. We have the occasional apple orchard, a rich rocky woods or two, perhaps a dead elm in a floodplain, or, just because they can do this as well, old bark mulch. So when they appear, which does not happen every year, those of us 'in the know' rejoice and celebrate. This second attempt at underscoring their mystique was better rewarded than the first!

PS. And no, I will not reveal my friend's name or even the town in which he lives!

Fluttering Mud

There it was again,
A fluttering in the mud.
No trick to the eye this time,
No poltergeist dud.
Looking closer, a waving of wings, and lift off…
Black-and-yellow, yellow-and-black,
Thank goodness, it looks like the swallowtail's back.
Immaculate tigery sheen
Scales magnificently cast,
The hindwing border a lush blue-green,
A butterfly's life is over way too fast.
One million spots of brilliance
Crafted from sugar and dirt,
Scales making flight impossibly light,
A frolicking flowery flirt.
Why do those minerals taste so fine?
A salty brew I've never tried,
Nor swallowed with tongue so long and refined,
A butterfly's salty nectar.
Is it the black or the yellow those salts impart,
To create such magnificence, such spectacular art,
Or is it the blues or greens or reds they've divined,
That arise inside those acrylic lines?
I cannot help but think it true,
If I were a butterfly I'd mimic you,
For finer feather-like wings cannot be found
This side of darkness upon the ground.

This was inspired by this sight of one of those never-old natural mysteries that I've witnessed since a young child – the "mudding" of tiger swallowtail butterflies. For those who have not witnessed this remarkable event, it occurs soon after the swallowtails emerge from their winter's cocoons, whereupon they smell, find, and feast on some aggregation of minerals in the dirt, mud, or feces along roadsides, beaches, skid trails, etc. With a rapid fluttering of wings, these two-gram denizens of forest and field flock together of up to, and sometimes exceeding, one hundred individuals (!). This particular 'mud party' was witnessed along a streambank far from roads, houses and the like, and so had that extra element of surprise and wonder. Watching the working of so many tongues was no less fascinating than the splatter of yellow and black as they lifted off and circled me on closer approach.

Just When You Thought

There is a customary sadness about change.
No furtive dribble here, just a passing remorse.
A forest I have known has been cut down,
Not, apparently, for any particular "improvement," or even
    for very much cash,
But because someone decided to do so.
Solid sugar maples standing tall,
Butternuts and basswoods
Everyone took the fall.
Nothing left, but a little debris here and there.
No bark for gleaning,
No snags for denning,
No twigs for nest building,
No buds for spring munching,
No flowers for pollinating,
No mast for consuming,
Only roots to sprout back,
Saplings to hack,
Fungi have the upperhand now,
Infiltrating wood everywhere,
Sending nutrients here and there,
Deprived of all but deadwood and air.
Who walks now on this hollow ground?
A fleeting visitor perhaps, that looks around,
No home is worth the tarry here,
All barren, sterile, and full of fear.
T'will be a long time before life regains
Its foothold within this forest's refrain,

Those who remember will be long gone away,
Chainsaws silent for yet another day,
Machines moving on, dollars on the run,
The rebuilding of respect for our forests has not yet begun.

This poem came to mind after walking up a very familiar trail on public land that was immediately adjacent to a 15-acre clearcut on private land. Having walked up this trail countless times, I was struck by the dramatic change in the forest's appearance, even on the uncut side. Light streamed in everywhere, the surface was bone dry in spite of the rainy spring, the birds were silent. As has been common of late, very little woody debris was left in the cut area, all of it having been whole-tree harvested. That which was left were all small branches between the stumps, most of which would succumb to fungal decomposition within about five years. After that, nothing. The forest itself would not be providing any substantial woody downfall for at least 15 years, and nothing of consequential size for at least 65 – 70 years. Late successional decompositional debris would not be available for wildlife or fungi for at least 175 – 250 years, and old growth conditions, with all of its complexity and micro-habitat diversity would not return for at least 450 – 550 years. It is very unlikely, barring a major economic collapse or other global upheaval of some sort that the next harvest rotation would wait for old growth conditions to re-appear before being exacted on this forest. And in the meanwhile?

Peek-a-boo Porky

At first glance
A hairy stance
Between rock and plant and tree,
Slowly then
A shaggy 'pig pen'
Took stock and ran from me,
But running hence
Into rocky fence
Could not effect escape,
Its eyes went wide
Looking side to side
Then stared me in the face.
A cautious look
From its rocky nook
With naught but eyes above,
This prickly clown
With grizzly gown
 Gave safety a little shove,
With stomping feet
And a foreboding bleat
It clambered closer still,
Like a miniature bear
Protecting its lair
Tail swishing every quill,
I was taken aback
By this unexpected tack
But stood my ground while whispering,
"You have naught to fear

From this curious seer
Whilst your coat stays sharp and glistening,
Why not rest here a while
And study my smile,
Let me do all the listening?"
And so it became
A peek-a-boo game
Of eyes and gentle whining,
It looked around, then nestled down
And took twig for casual dining,
It lost interest in me and who I could be
As it went back to porcupining.

This light-hearted poem was inspired by an encounter with a porcupine, one of several dozen I typically have during a given year. Yet this was a little different in that the individual stood its ground and began stomping and whining from its rocky retreat. The small porcupine scat nearby hinted at the fact that this individual was likely a *she* and *she* was likely defending her young who were otherwise ensconced in the rocky defile below. Here periodic peering above a boulder suggested a 'peek-a-boo' game as she checked my position from time to time. After a while, this guarding behavior stopped and she went back to doing what any normal porcupine would do, eating, resting, and rustling about.

Bluebird Wake-up Call

Consciousness crept in on a smile,
Though sleep was but a little while,
Cheerful song for a misty dawn,
As if it were still a dream.

What power lay in that melody,
A 'cheer-cheerful-charmer' parody,
A survivor of quiet fields and DDT,
Long gone but not forgotten.

Now all the bird boxes are filled,
With a soft and tremulous trill,
The bluebird's note I now know by rote,
Bringing dawn into the light.

That smile on my face was born from a former disgrace
With the greed of humankind,
When chemicals lined the pockets of suits
And people were heartlessly blind.

I care less the thought of birds we have lost
Than of those we can still recover,
For bluebirds and hawks, grosbeaks and auks
Need more than just one another.

The conscientious gain of a bluebird's refrain
Lies not in its own resounding,
Rather it lies in a much bigger prize—
The symphony of all life rebounding.

This morning I awoke to a bluebird's wonderfully cheerful call. It began what would otherwise be another trying day where news of the world brought into sharp focus the stupidity of people and their treatment of the environment. The pronouncement by the American President that we would withdraw from the Paris Climate Accord, signed by over 164 nations, put a damper on this beautiful spring day. It reminded me of how business interests and greed forced DDT upon the world and nearly wiped out a number of bird species, including the bluebird. Only the cries of those who cared, the Rachel Carsons of the world, brought this reign of terror to an end. While we are still not without a vast array of noxious chemicals that we apply regularly to the Earth, we have at least forestalled the demise of the bluebird, and in fact, helped bring about its return with a proliferation of box building enterprises that has just barely assuaged the guilt of our past misdeeds.

The Four Kings

Standing there you are,
Since Paradise Lost was first published in a faraway land,
Swaying back and forth
Witnessing
The passing of centuries.
All four of you have bowed your heads in this passing
Having long since gained the Sun's breath
And touched the Earth's core
Deeply rooted in solid rock.
As kings you cared not for Religion
Or Faith
Or Knowledge,
For yours has been the kingdom of being still
Living every moment in place
Through wind and storm and heat
Nurturing countless generations of birds,
Feeding thousands of four-leggeds with your food,
Watering millions of mosses with your moisture,
Enriching lichen and root, fungus and herb
With the drippings, the raining of time flowing eternal.

My great kings how you have stood
In solemn salute to those who otherwise would,
Take you down for post and beam,
Yet those you carry not,
For lightening has scarred you,
Borne rot inside you,
And thundered out a hollow of a bear's den dream.

You have watched four cycles of Haley's treat,
The aborigines in full retreat,
The coming of the British fleet,
The loss of your wooded friends cut down and beat,
The summer with very little heat,
The Union soldier maiden's entreat,
The vacating of the shepherd's seat,
And the return of rifle hunted meat.

Yet, and yet
So perfectly set on this glorious mountainside stage,
Your arms outstretched
With oaken wisdom and sage
Advice to the weary, to those who might tarry,
And listen to your hearts,
Feel your warm embrace,
Finding comfort in knowing still,
You long to live on this mountain until,
The time has come for you to rot away,
And bear acorns to live another age.

The four 'kings' were mighty oaks, each exceeding 300 years in age, with girths of four feet or more, standing as a group of silent sentinels in a forested wood. These were on the side of a well-known mountain in my home state, not particularly unique but solemnly wise for having survived, provided, and sustained the vagaries of time. Touching their bark I could almost feel their age and wisdom being passed on, certainly in the pausing an opportunity to reflect on the ephemeral nature of our generational bias as humans, who buffer ourselves from the harsh realities of the world with our own trappings of comfort and self-servitude.

Tracking Sense

Watching my dog use her nose—
Ancient survival art inclined,
The ball, like so many prey species before,
Succumbs to pounce and grip.

I wonder now in quiet repose,
How many olfactory cells we have lost,
How many survival instincts have become extinct,
And at what cost?

Tracking seems so very basic to me,
Yet to most, an odd "sport" if you can call it that,
Brushed on with camouflage and heavy doses of deet,
Complete with rifle and arm
No more nose-to-the-ground, owl calls of alarm,
Our four-legged ancestors long since forgotten.

No, tracking now, befits stockholders and investors,
Wall Streeters and marketers,
Looking at screen after screen of numbers, more numbers
Preying on prices,
Ravashing on returns,
Gorging on global greed and gluttony.

No, this is not for me,
Tracking is still a fine art of survival –
Survival from our inescapable tendency to forget
Everything we have evolved to become,

Everything we know we could be and, perhaps, should be,
Everything our ancestors left us in the wake of their own
    sacrifices,
Everything our biophilic instincts have taught us to use
Everything, simply
Everything.

What sense is it then to walk through the world blind?
To smell naught but perfume and money?
To taste only sweet, or fatty meat?
To see the world through a screen?
To hear only the noise of our own mutterings
About how much we don't own,
How much we can't control,
How much we have lost, and
How much we can't become.

No, tracking is now more urgent than ever before,
To listen to my ancestors whispering in my ear,
To hear the grumbling stomach of a bear in its den,
To see the stars beyond the stars and all in between,
To feel bare earth between my toes,
To sharpen everything,
Every glance
Every smell,
Every sound,
Every taste,
Every touch,
Every sense, yes, tracking above all is to make sense of
    making sense.

This poem was inspired by my dog, Addie, who smells everything ten or twenty times better than me. It is also inspired by al the dogs I have known, who have brought in close to their world of scent, casting aside sight for the olfactory delight. I have imagined a few hundred more brain cells devoted to such neural responses, and yet have also realized that not all is lost in humans, and that in fact the nose can be "awakened" to recognize a lot more than we think. As such, I have learned to recognize the difference between male and female fox, a coyote in estrus, a moose scent two days versus one day old, deer scents by season and in rut, the body odor of bear, the smell of moose in fear, the fine perfumery of fisher females in heat. I hold no special code for this ability, just time and practice. To all of my dogs everywhere, I devote this poem to their senses.

Journeying On

A flight of nighthawks went by
Cutting wings through darkened sky,
On their way home again.
Dozens swarmed over field and forest,
Capturing insects, a flying bug fest,
On their way home again.
Six thousand miles they've come,
Slicing their way across the sun,
Continent to continent, driven to be
On their way home again.

I used to dream of nighthawks,
Flying o'er mountains and the sea,
Swiftly diving then gaining ground
Feathered fletching covering me,
Goat-suckers all around,
A life as Caprimulgidae.

But my ancestors broke the arboreal mold,
Descending from tree, making fire against cold,
Running fast, chasing prey
So far from the fold, so very far from the fold,
Earning the right to be free.

And so now I wander without home ingrained,
Weary from the travel, a little bit strained,
Wondering where my wings will next rest,
And where I will build my casual nest.

118 • Crossing Paths for 45 Days

I envy the nighthawks from a distant land,
Who know exactly where they stand,
As nighthawks should with an avian code,
Hard-wired to choose a certain abode,
Unlike those of us who have forgotten our kin,
And selected to pretend we know where to begin,
Yet troubled for wont of returning from afar
To the very same home, like an elegant nightjar,
Ours is but to sample a new dawn,
And carry our spirit as we journey on.

This poem was inspired by witnessing a pair of nighthawks as they migrated north to breeding grounds in northern New Hampshire or southern Canada. It brought back quick memories of one day late last August, when I saw a nighthawk spectacle of unimaginable proportions – hundreds of hawking birds over an intervale at dusk. Though I've seen many a nighthawk migration, and have timed my outdoors viewing to correspond with their peak flight periods, I had never in 50 years of bird-watching all over the world seen as many Caprimulgids in one spot. The fact that that many had converged in one locale after having spent much of the summer alone or in small groups at their breeding ground was impressive. Even more impressive was the fact that these same birds will split apart again near their wintering grounds, returning typically to the very same wintering locale, and then repeat the process once again in the spring.

Conclusion

It is the hope of this author that these poems inspire you to go out and explore Nature in all of its complex simplicity. There is so much of the Earth to see and experience. It is truly a remarkable planet, filled with secrets and stories we have only begun to interpret. Although we humans have indelibly altered the landscape within which we live, we are still able to marvel at its intricacies and delight in its beauty. So much of life it seems, lives on without us, without even the faintest idea that we exist. Whether it be a bright yellow flower in the sunlight, a chorusing peeper at twilight, or a couple of playful bears, there are always aspects of Nature to observe and appreciate.

The more we observe and experience the natural world, the more we realize it is at once a dynamic, survivalistic, and somewhat fragile place. In a pure Darwinian sense, the fittest survive. And yet, how often does fitness beget cooperation, companionship, and community? It appears that the very basis of survival is dependent upon an ability to adapt *with others*, and that by understanding others we too can perfect our own survival.

To some, perfecting our own survival depends on our promotion of *Resilience*, yet the concept of resilience is an artifact of our own misgivings. We have embodied this word with a meaning that assumes a) we actually understand how the world works, and b) that we can do something about it. It may come as a surprise to you that these are utterly false assumptions. That said, it should not stop any or all of your well–intentioned efforts to keep trying to understand our world and take actions that help mitigate the effects of our footprint upon it.

To most of us who believe 'we have but one life to live,' there is no better time to act than the present. It is all too easy to settle in to a life style that is comfortable, that is easy, and offers little challenge to our survivalist roots. This is not to say that we need to get undressed, grab a knife, and head off into the nearest wilderness. What it does mean is that there is always an opportunity—*every day*—to make one choice, one decision, one action to improve our world in a demonstrable way. Buy locally, bike to work, drive an electric vehicle, get involved in community. There are a million ways to respect the planet—*our* Home. So why not start now?

Acknowledgments

I would first like to recognize and thank all of the mentors who taught me about the natural world while growing up and in school. With encouragement from my grandparents, my mother, my twin brother, and my extended family members I was able to gain a great deal of insight and perspective. Dr. Willi Unsoeld encouraged me to believe in the impossible, Mr. Freeman Rowe introduced me to the intricacies of fungal and floral world, and Dr. Harry Thiers demonstrated exceptional teaching methods and gave me the confidence to begin my professional teaching career. To these fine people I owe a debt of gratitude. Finally, and without hesitation I can say that my wife Wendy, an accomplished author in her own right (now working on her 8th book), gave me the encouragement and guidance to undertake such an endeavor in the first place. This book would not have been possible without her steadfast sense of "just do it!"

About the Author

Dr. Van de Poll enters the field of poetry writing as an experienced ecologist and seasoned science writer. While he has authored and co-authored a number of technical works on the science of nature, this book is his first foray into poetry writing. He comes with a keen eye for the natural world, wherein his first-hand experiences across Central and North America and Europe has provided him with a wealth of knowledge about flora, fauna, and the nature of diverse ecosystems. With degrees in Outdoor Education, Mycology, Environmental Communication and Natural Resource Management, Rick has taught at the undergraduate and graduate level for over thirty years and has offered hundreds of workshops, seminars and classes in a large number of natural resource topics. As an environmental science consultant, he has worked in all parts of North America and selected locales in Mexico and Italy. He has undertaken and completed comprehensive ecological inventories of over 300,000 acres in 85 towns in New Hampshire, Vermont, Maine, Massachusetts, and New York. He currently is the Principal of Ecosystem Management Consultants and can be reached at www.rickvandepoll.com .

CPSIA information can be obtained
at www.ICGtesting.com
Printed in the USA
LVHW031530220121
677171LV00003B/198